LAKE / FLATO

Foreword by
William Turnbull, F.A.I.A.

Introduction by
Richard Brettell

Concept and Design by
Lucas H. Guerra
Oscar Riera Ojeda

ROCKPORT PUBLISHERS
GLOUCESTER, MASSACHUSETTS

First published in the United States of America by:
Rockport Publishers, Inc.
33 Commercial Street
Gloucester, Massachusetts 01966
Telephone: (978) 282-9590
Fax: (978) 283-2742

Distribution by:
Rockport Publishers, Inc.
Gloucester, Massachusetts 01966

ISBN 1-56496-233-4

10 9 8 7 6 5 4 3 2 1

Graphic Design: Lucas H. Guerra/ Oscar Riera Ojeda
Connexus Visual Communications/ Boston
Layout: Oscar Riera Ojeda
Mechanicals: Javier Huerta
Editor: Don Fluckinger
Project Descriptions: Ray Don Tilley
Cover Photo: Carraro Residence
© Hester+Hardaway Photography, Fayetteville, Texas
Back Cover Photos: (Top) Burlington Northern Santa Fe by
Michael Lyon and (Bottom) Great Northwest Branch Library
© Hester+Hardaway Photography, Fayetteville, Texas

Printing in Hong Kong
by Midas Printing Limited

CONTENTS

Foreword

BY WILLIAM TURNBULL, F.A.I.A.

David Lake and Ted Flato are architects. They are not scenery designers or architectural tailors. They make thoughtful buildings that consider space and light and the tough climate of their native Southwest. They site buildings sensitively in an unforgiving Texas landscape and build them of elegantly crafted, commonplace materials. They are not fashion followers—their buildings are not "dressed" to respond to the latest architectural fads and they are not particularly concerned with what the taste-makers are doing. This is why they are important architects.

In the United States there is a long tradition of elegant architecture sometimes by noted names like Thomas Jefferson, and sometimes by unknown craftsmen builders like those who built the Pennsylvania bank barns. As the country grew and moved west, common-sense construction and innovative problem solving left a legacy of well loved buildings. The heavy timber frames of the wood-plentiful East gave way to the light stick construction of the Midwest and evolved into the "soddies" of the Nebraska plains when there was no wood to be had. In the Southwest the adobe dirt, or *caliche*, provided unlimited amounts of building material and hundreds of years of thick-walled architecture resulted.

With the formalized arrival of architectural schools in the East, the carpenter, craftsman architect was superseded by the professionals who, under the influence of the Beaux Arts, were purveyors of style but educated to the harmonies of proportion, detail and elegant materials. What the Beaux Arts did to the visual expression of construction technology, the Modern Movement did to the efficacy of site-specific architectural solutions. Frank Lloyd Wright stood in the middle of the country decrying both and espousing the landscape and its natural materials. All the while, farmers, ranchers and folks on the frontier built away, solving problems with materials at hand, letting comfort and common sense be their guides, without the benefit of professional assistance.

In Texas, after the Second War, young O'Neil Ford set out in San Antonio to find his own version of the contextual vernacular. Lessons from the local masonry building tradition were absorbed and reborn in his buildings. Questions of habitation and comfortability in the rigorous climate were explored. He spent his life energetically pursuing and sharing his insights about the cultural, climatic and material opportunities of Texas with those he worked for and those who worked with him. These are the roots of Ted Flato and David Lake. In 1981, the two young architects met in O'Neil Ford's office and matured under the umbrella of his ideas and concerns for an appropriate Texas architecture.

No architect can shake his past like dust from his boots: where he was born and played as a child, ideas learned and shared at the University, buildings he has seen, things he has read. These all go to form a lexicon of hopes and dreams and desires that merge into insights and then become buildings for others.

In the case of these two, Lake and Flato, they have specifically Texas insights but the quality of their translation into architecture can serve as lesson for us all: how a building stands to the sun, how it welcomes the cooling breeze, how it partners with plant materials: these are lessons in siting. Appropriate construction materials are important so the structure marries with the site: corregated iron to turn the heat, heavy stone or adobe to shelter the occupants, light frame for the support of shady porches, cool tile for floors underfoot. Nothing sensational or exotic, no visual fireworks of fashion, just architecture that intrigues the mind, delights the soul, and refreshes the eye with its elegant detail and simplicity.

Timeless architecture needn't shout; in south Texas, it is more pleasant to listen to the wind whispering through it.

Introduction

BY RICHARD BRETTEL

Ascending a dozen or so steps to the mirador of La Estrella Ranch, an early Lake/Flato project, the vast Texas landscape unfurls. In the distance among gentle rises, clumps of mesquite, and verdant creek paths traced in the dry earth are century-old structures, bleached and abstracted by high sun. These buildings recall Texas' various settlers: Indians, who cut pathways and left early structures; the Spanish and French, who built missions, forts, and communities; and Germans, who erected wood and stone dwellings in the 1800s. The railroad era brought brick architecture, cotton's reign introduced metal gins and warehouses, and the early 20th century left austere, geometric industrial and agricultural buildings. Salient examples from this heterogeny of building remain, and their shapes, materials, and siting pervade the sensibilities of David Lake and Ted Flato.

Both Lake and Flato grew up in Texas. David Lake received a bachelor's degree in architecture from the University of Texas at Austin in 1976. Inspired by professor Pliny Fisk's sustainable designs, he moved to the Panhandle and built modern sod-buster houses for farmers who enjoyed the notion of cows grazing on the roof. Ted Flato earned a bachelor's degree in Architecture from Stanford University, where he absorbed William Turnbull's enthusiastic sensitivity to site and context. Ted returned to his ancestral roots in Central Texas and began applying these principles in the design of goat pens, houses, and a small-town bank.

David Lake and Ted Flato met in 1981 under the watchful eye of O'Neil Ford, the most articulate and passionate Texas architect of mid-20th century. Ford practiced what can be called vernacular modernism and perfected its expression in universities, schools, museums, and, most memorably, houses. His office was a laboratory for young architects who loved Mexico as much as Texas, who visited and restored 18th- and 19th-century buildings, and who championed Luis Barragan long before the Museum of Modern Art did.

At Ford Powell and Carson in San Antonio, Ford paired Flato with Lake, who had arrived two years before. Ford whispered to Lake, "Thinks he's a good designer; [I] want you to knock the chip off, straighten him out." The young architects clashed immediately on the design of a bank in Boerne: Ted saw a flat roof, square windows; David, a pitched roof, arches. The bank's board chose a blend of both visions; from that meeting forward, they would work together, spiritedly, much as they do today.

(Opposite page) From La Estrella's mirador (lookout), Andrew Lake views to the mountains north of Monterrey, Mexico. (Top) Lake/Flato's Fair Oaks Bank is a good example of how the architects combine light industrial forms with massive grounded masonry walls to create a contrast of spatial experience to bring the outdoors into their buildings.

 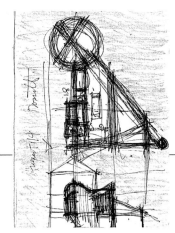

Their partnership rests on a love of similar architecture and divergent—but complementary—problem solving. Ted designs with great resolve, evolving project by project. David works intuitively, with studied analysis leading to invention. Both draw inspiration from the site and client, each directing the projects that appeal to him while working with the other as critic and collaborator. Ten years have brought buildings that equal the works by Ford and others past: simple, solid structures extending the architectural lineage of a modern vernacular.

This solid architecture ages gracefully, settling with its site, within the regional climate and character of buildings that have responded well to the surroundings, with easily discerned forms and clear functions. Design proceeds with far-sighted ideals in mind, to merge soil, trees, sun, and breezes with local traditions, craftsmen, and materials. With study and response—tapping a wellspring of forms and materials, archaic and modern—the natural qualities of the site and building coalesce. In Texas, for example, the word "cool" has all the richness and appeal that the word "warm" does in Chicago or New England. A cooling Texas breeze, once found, must be cleverly diverted through rooms. Or consider light, which in Texas is as destructive as it is revelatory of architectural form. It blinds, heats, fades, and weathers architecture with a force so tangible that Lake/Flato often creates spaces with boundaries that evade it, modify it, and even deny it. In selecting materials, the firm honors gravity's unrelenting power, using limestone, caliche block, brick, and stucco to extend the examples of yesterday's builders by anchoring to the landscape the light building systems of today.

The buildings in this, the firm's first monograph, range from a suburban corporate headquarters to recycled warehouses, a reborn state cemetery, and seven ranch houses. Its four works-in-progress display a flowering in scale and variety among the firm's building types and sites. The work of Lake/Flato Architects has assumed and perpetuated the fertile legacy of Ford and his progenitors: a modern architecture rising from traditions, crafts, and forms suited to the site. The body of work is mostly in Texas, yet Lake/Flato's principles and attitudes are not confined to the state. Japan, as the Lasaters' house suggests, offers fertile inspiration, as do the materials at hand in New Mexico and Colorado, where projects are under way. Their vocabulary continues to grow, and the process of assimilating climate, character, and the dreams of dozens of individual clients continues to advance an architecture of both modern technology and the soul of a region's enduring vernacular buildings.

Hogwild is a rural retreat inspired by Central Texas cotton warehouses, gins, and silos. The third-floor deck floats in the landscape, while beyond the porch a clerestory pops up from the shed roof for views to the horizon.

Works ▶

Santa Fe House I

In Santa Fe's Historic District, this piñon-covered site slopes downhill between two old adobe houses, away from the street, toward the northern views. The client wanted a small house that "has the charm and permanence of an old adobe but somehow is filled with light and space." The historic building codes required squat massing, stucco exterior materials, and small recessed windows; to these dictates, Lake/Flato applied passive solar technology.

The house digs into the land six feet on the uphill side to provide earth sheltering and to present a low profile to the street. In addition to a mostly wood-frame and stucco structure, three sculptural adobe elements define space and circulation while providing thermal mass for passive solar heating. On hot days, the mass of the walls insulates the interior, and careful ventilation assures a breeze. In winter, light entering through a south-facing clerestory strikes the adobe and warms the space. One wall, forming a truncated kiva—the ceremonial space of local ancient dwellings—curves around the library from the front door into the forty-foot-long living room. The triangular fireplace bisects this room into living and dining spaces, similar to fireplaces found in New Mexico Territorial homes. Pine beams and wood decking enliven ceilings, while gauging plaster lends a feeling of permanence to interiors walls. The forced-perspective "stair to the sky" leads to the sunset deck and is illuminated during the day by the solar clerestory. Continual movement past the mud sculptures and the play of light upon them give this house its spirit.

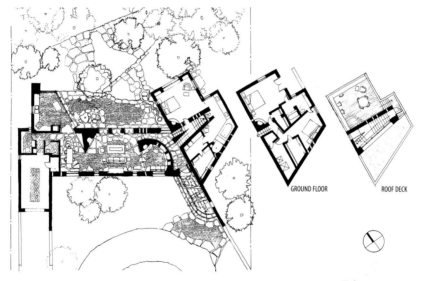

GROUND FLOOR   ROOF DECK

A temperature of 58 degrees is maintained in the winter without additional heat sources, because the adobe acts as a passive solar heat conductor; a temperature of 70 degrees in the summer is maintained without air-conditioning. (Below) A recycled Mexican jail door is filled with multi-colored glass to become the front door.

La Barronena Ranch

For many years, the Lasater family spent its weekends camping in tents and cooking out in the arid brush country of their South Texas ranch, La Barronena, near Hebbronville. When they decided to build a house, the Lasaters did not want to lose the feeling of being close to the land. They turned to the architectural firm of Ford Powell & Carson, where Principal in Charge Chris Carson led a team that included Ted Flato.

La Barronena sits on a gentle ridge amid the wild brush and gnarled mesquite trees of the South Texas plains just inland from the Gulf of Mexico. It is a harsh landscape, tempered by ever-present coastal breezes. Recalling the archetypal low-slung Texas barn, with wide, low-sloped, corrugated-metal-covered roofs extending out from a steeper-pitched central space, this project centers on a central volume built from stuccoed concrete block and containing an indoor kitchen. Spaces are organized to capture the tent-like feeling of outdoor living. Informal, screened-in living areas and open porches circle the kitchen and extend as covered breezeways to the two stuccoed sleeping quarters at either end of the house. In summer, the southerly breeze wafts through the porches, and a high, central cupola with operable louvers draws the cool air up through the interior kitchen. A small, L-shaped lake constructed on the windward side of the house enhances the cooling effect of the breeze and tempers the hot, expansive landscape. In winter, massive, rolling barn doors extend across the breezeways to block the harsh north winds. The kitchen is enclosed by thick storage walls, creating a strong sense of shelter.

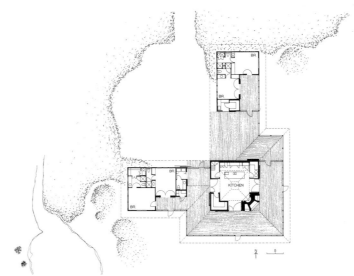

(Opposite page, above) The late 19th-century Fort Davis Infirmary serves as a lesson in "dog-runs." Dog-runs are Texas breezeways which separate living and sleeping areas, funneling breezes through both. (Bottom) Wide openings in the thick storage walls allow the central kitchen to merge with the surrounding screen porch.

South Burke Ranch

ZAVALA COUNTY, TEXAS

As they did with the much larger La Estrella Ranch, Lake/Flato found inspiration in the spare, small-scaled brick, stone, and stucco buildings of the lower Rio Grande Valley towns of Roma and Guerrero for their design of South Burke Ranch Headquarters. South Burke's simpler form fits its small scale and reflects the primitive, spare architectural influences of the region. Its emphasis on providing shade and melding with the environment creates an arbor house that serves as a cool retreat from the barren landscape and intensely hot summer temperatures.

Situated atop a gravel ridge, the U-shaped house opens to the southeast to capture the prevailing summer breezes and, with windows on the opposite facade, brings in views of the valley to the north. The three sides of the "U" are separate buildings connected by screened porches. The stucco-on-concrete-block buildings are only one room wide, ensuring excellent cross-ventilation. Inside, each structure contains one or more thick walls—enclosures that read as walls but conceal collections of small utilitarian spaces such as closets and bathrooms. Stucco carries through to interior walls, floors are sealed concrete, and pine beams and flat wood decking grace the ceilings. Surrounding the house are arbors covered with mustang grape vines. In a treeless setting, these arbors create a garden atmosphere that protects the house from the severe summer climate. In the winter, the vines lose their leaves and allow the sun's rays to penetrate the house, which provides warmth in cold weather. With their oversized column bases, the arbors tie the compound to the earth, creating a gradual transition from site to building.

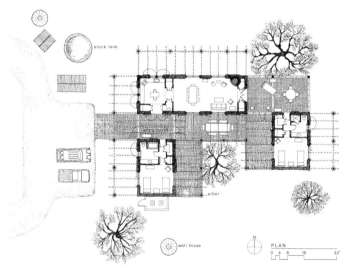

(Opposite page, above) Late 19th-century gabled parapet buildings are common along the Rio Grande River, and Lake/Flato has long admired their clarity of form. The arbors wrap the house and provide shade from the summer sun, and in places the arbors become screened porches.

La Estrella Ranch

ROMA, TEXAS

"I want the house to look as though it's been here for a hundred years," said Tommy Funk, owner of La Estrella ranch, located north of Roma, Texas, thirty miles from the Rio Grande River. Mr. Funk has lived in the Rio Grande Valley all his life and always admired 19th-century brick buildings in nearby Roma and Rio Grande City. Lake/Flato adopted brick details from these structures, such as recessed wall panels, pilasters, and cornices, to create a village of Funk's favorite buildings.

The headquarters compound sits on a rise amid mesquite, wild olive, and Texas ebony trees near the center of a large semi-arid ranch. Trees and shade are rare commodities in this region, so, in the manner of a northern Mexico hacienda, the buildings round up the trees into a courtyard bounded by porches, breezeways, walls, and cisterns. To the existing main house and partial guest wing Lake/Flato added a guest room with interior boveda (domed ceiling), mirador(roof deck), north wall, the master quarters, and a game room/barbecue area. New construction was clad in low-fired Mexican brick, which varies widely in porosity and hardness. Fresh paints, mixed from powdered Mexican pigments, were applied throughout, creating a cohesive palette that weathers and peels to an ancient appearance identical to the old buildings Funk so loves. The central courtyard captures cooling southeast winds from the Gulf of Mexico with its breezeways and porches. In the winter, colder north winds are deflected over the courtyard walls. The fifteen-foot-deep porches serve as outdoor rooms for dining and entertaining ten months of the year.

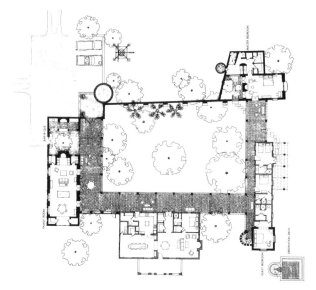

(Opposite page, above) This Rio Grande City building was one of Mr. Funk's favorites. The outdoor shower looks like a cistern, walls out rattlesnakes, and provides good sky viewing. Materials from Mexico were incorporated into the design. *Bovedas* (flat brick domes), unpainted clinker brick, face brick, and pavers came from a Mexican kiln 30 miles away.

La Estrella Ranch

Cornices, recessed wall panels, and
arched inglenooks provide detail to
the simple brick buildings. A variety
of roof heights, breezeways, and
buildings create an interesting porch
experience. The hacienda walls keep
the cool air trapped in the courtyard.

① PARAPET DETAIL - LIVING ROOM
  NOT TO SCALE

② PARAPET DETAIL - PORCH BETWEEN
  GUEST HOUSE &
  LIVING ROOM

STANDARDS AND REGULATIONS:

Applicable standards of construction industry and Building Codes
have the same force and effect on performance of the work as
if copied directly into contract documents. Governing regulations
have precedence over nonreferenced standards, in so far as
different standards may contain overlapping or conflicting
requirements. Comply with local Building Codes and Industry
Standards. Contractor is responsible for compliance with these
standards and regulations and for the construction permits.

The installation shall meet the minimum standards prescribed in
the latest edition of the following standards:

1. UPC 70 Uniform   Plumbing Code
2. NFPA No. 70-1978   National Electric Code
3. NEMA standards for installation
4. Uniform Mechanical Code 1986

All mechanical, electrical, and plumbing indicated on drawings is
simply to aid contractor on general locations. The contractor
is responsible for electrical, plumbing and mechanical sizing, and
shall adhere to these codes.

③ SECTION - INTERIOR ELEVATION
  1/4"

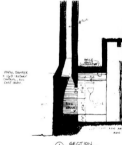

④ SECTION
  1/4"

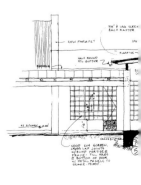

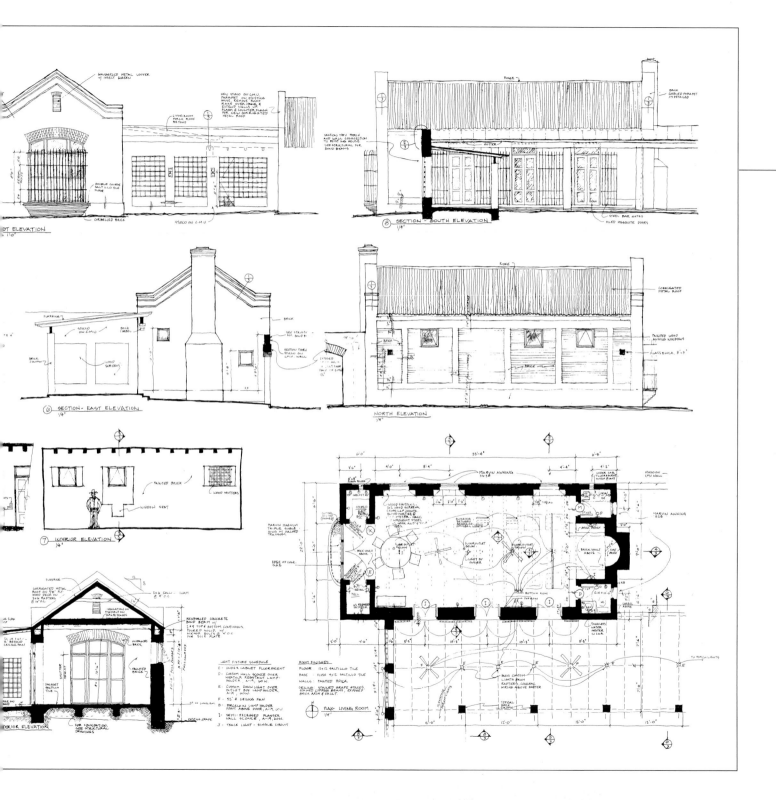

Carter Ranch

MILLICAN, TEXAS

A hundred miles northwest of Houston, the Brazos River Valley, a green landscape of rolling hills and oak trees scattered in small groves or standing majestically alone, provided a pleasant setting for the Carter Ranch house. The cluster of buildings have the feel of an old farm: three sections form a horseshoe, while in the middle is a courtyard protected from the grazing cattle and shaded by a towering oak. Between the buildings, arbor-covered walkways allow the breeze to flow through the courtyard.

The structures, mostly stucco-on-wood-frame, have the rambling feel of a familiar Texas ranch compound, where an original homestead is added onto room by room, building by building, as needs arise. A two-story main house rises up with geometric clarity. Attached is a metal-clad volume containing stairs, kitchen, and bath, and a crisp, glass shed housing the living room. A guest house and garage, disguised as low-slung barns help frame the courtyard. The use of simple, inexpensive materials such as metal, pipe, wood, wire, and stucco capture the ranch vernacular while lending a new, light elegance to this traditional building type. The contrast of thin standing-seam-metal awnings and slender pipe supports with the massive stuccoed structures to which they are attached emphasizes the solidity and permanent feel of the main buildings.

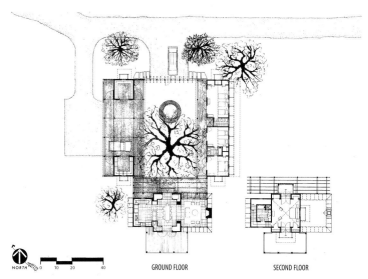

NORTH   0 10 20   40

GROUND FLOOR   SECOND FLOOR

A variety of overhangs, flaps, and arbors cast shadow upon the building. Sliding galvanized metal barn doors cover the cars while uncovering a connection to the courtyard. Hogwire is attached to the wood arbors to encourage vines to cover them.

In the main house, the dining room acts as a central entry hall, with openings to its four adjacent spaces: the kitchen, the living room, the front door and the main courtyard.

El Tule Ranch

FALFURRIAS, TEXAS

On the sandy coastal plains of South Texas, groves of large oak and mesquite trees only occasionally interrupt an endless horizon of golden, flowing grasses. Lake/Flato chose one such shady dune as the site for the primary residence and headquarters for the owners of El Tule Ranch. Tucked among the sprawling trees, the house becomes part of the landscape. Even the soil was used as a building material: local caliche was quarried and pressed into mud blocks for the walls.

As a contrast to the wide-open views, the architects created a series of pavilions that ring a lush and exuberant courtyard filled with flowering plants. The clients wanted their house both to frame views of the surrounding environment and to turn inward on a private garden landscape. At the center of the courtyard, a long, narrow pool not only recalls the use of water at the Alhambra in Spain, but also serves as an acequia (irrigation canal) to water the garden with the rain it catches. Adjacent to the courtyard is the caretaker's house: a simple, shed-like structure with its own oak court.

Buildings open to unobstructed southeasterly breezes, while a long masonry north wall shields the compound and its gardens from winter winds. Looking outward, El Tule offers the unobstructed open horizon, while inward views offer both respite and drama.

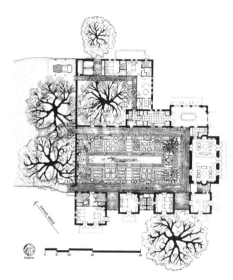

Protected by two giant oaks, the main entrance of the house leads through a long wall to a lush interior courtyard. The beds of flowering plants are organized by irrigation canals used to water the gardens. Guest-room pavilions are connected by the porch and gridded breezeways.

(Opposite page) All the rooms capture the two contrasting worlds: the fertile courtyard within and the expansive grasslands beyond. The walled court keeps out blustery coastal winds and wildlife so the lush plants may flourish. (Above) A series of "flaps," broad over-hangs supported by pipe brackets, work as private porches, protecting the doorways along the perimeter of the house.

1" STUCCO
FLASHING
CORRUGATED MET. ROOF
2×4's @ 16" o.c.
4×4 (BEYOND)

12
A·10

4 | 12

TWO NEOPRENE
CLOSURE STRIPS -
CONTINUOUS

1¼" I.D. GALV. PIPE
SUPPORTS

CONTIN. 1¼" I.D. GALV.
PIPE W/ "KEE KLAMP"
NO. 70-7 SUPPORT W/ 84-7 PLUG

"KEE KLAMP" NO. 10-7
SINGLE SOCKET TEE

"KEE KLAMP"
NO. C58-7

6'-0"

SECTION THRU FLAP
SCALE : 1½" = 1'-0"

2×4 @ 16" o.c.
CORRUGATED MET. ROOF

4×4

"KEE KLAMP" NO. 70-7
"KEE KLAMP" NO. 10-7

STUCCO OPENING
@ WINDOW

2'-0"   1'-0"

DETAIL @ FLAP
SCALE : 1½" = 1'-0"

Salge Lake House

On this narrow, tree-covered lot on Canyon Lake, thirty miles north of San Antonio, the client wanted to build an economical weekend house that could accommodate numerous guests. Flanked on two sides by other houses, with the lakefront down the hill, site constraints suggested a plan that closed off side views and emphasized the axial view from the front door through the house to the lake. Lake/Flato designed the nine-hundred-square-foot house as a big, barn-like room with exterior and interior walls that border three sides of the great room creating cavities between the inner and outer "shells" of the building large enough to hold four bedrooms, two bathrooms, and storage. These "thick walls" also act as blinders to the east and west, focusing the view toward a shallow, two-story screened porch facing the lake. With its dramatic concrete stair, the large space functions simultaneously as a grand entry hall, a screened pavilion, and a living/dining/kitchen room. Stucco-on-wood-frame walls, concrete floors, and a corrugated metal roof met the client's desire for economy.

The main room is designed for all seasons. During the warm months, with the 12-foot-tall doors open, the house functions as a large screened pavilion oriented to the cool prevailing breezes from the lake. The central cupola and the upper interior shutters enhance the natural ventilation. In cold months, when the glass doors are closed, the main room has a warm southern exposure. But it is the lake view, year round, that remains the dominant feature in this one-room house.

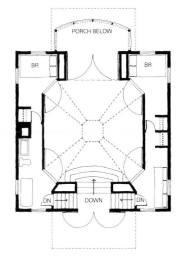

UPPER LEVEL PLAN

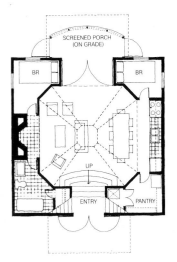

GROUND LEVEL PLAN

The architects used several elements to achieve an overall effect of an open hillside pavilion: grand concrete entry stairs allow the sloping site to flow through the main room; big doors open the two-story wall to the lake; exterior stucco is carried through the interior; and a central cupola brings in additional natural light while breaking up the ceiling. Designed with the efficiency of a boat, five bedrooms encircle the living space.

Chandler Ranch

MASON, TEXAS

Perched above the steep and rugged limestone bluff of the Llano River in Central Texas, the Chandler Ranch house melds into the rocky landscape while preserving the natural, sensitive beauty of the cliff. The view of the river and surrounding Hill Country drew the clients to this precarious peninsula of stone. Using the wonderfully rustic 1921 Glen Alpine Lodge by Bernard Maybeck as a spring board, Lake/Flato was able to demonstrate to the client that a house could be built along this rocky ridge without damaging or compromising the site.

To accommodate the steep grades and prevailing breezes, the house is designed in a narrow, linear fashion. A long, arcing entry porch creates a wide seating area at the midpoint of the bedroom wing and leads, through the kitchen, to the main octagonal pavilion that serves as a comfortable living room and year-round lookout. Weathered limestone collected from the ranch is stacked to create thick, sturdy corbelled piers that anchor the three-bedroom house to the site. Lighter, simpler forms hover among the buttresses and details—such as thin awnings made of recycled oil-field rods—lend a delicate grace and contrast with the heavy limestone. In fact, the massive stone buttresses here do as much as the oil-pipe shades to provide shelter from the sun while framing living room views to the outside, making the room feel as if it were part of the cliff.

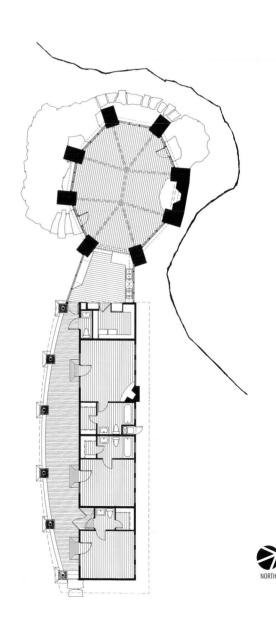

NORTH

The weathered stone for the buttress column footings was gathered from the site and laid in a "dry stacked" manner to emmulate the craggy texture of the adjacent cliff. The massive forms help connect the house to the barren hill side.

In the main rooms, the stone buttresses help frame the views of the cliffs of the Llano River as well as creating closure in the glass room. The octagonal living room with a Wrightian hearth and beamed ceiling is both a gathering space and lookout room.

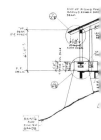

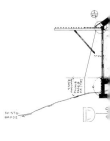

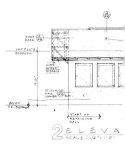

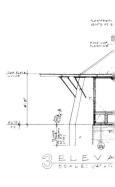

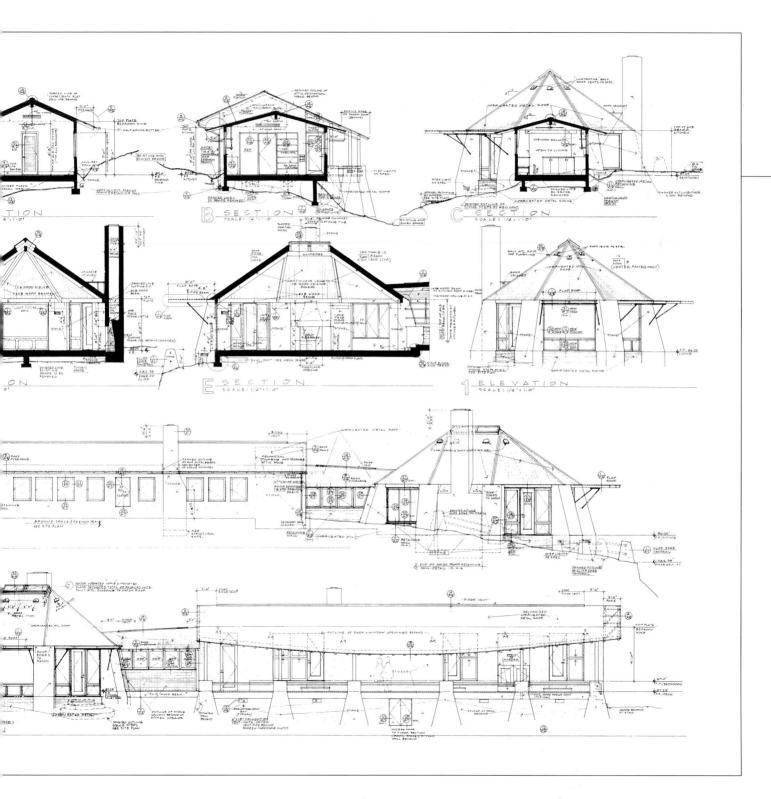

Cotulla Ranch

COTULLA, TEXAS

A lush riverbank and flat, arid brush country inspired the collection of forms for this South Texas ranch house. The main room, a light-steel-framed shelter, is anchored to the ever-changing riverbank by heavy stone buttresses. To forge a connection to the outdoors, the openings between the massive buttresses are sheathed in horizontal screen bands protected from inclement weather by large, operable glass shutters. The standing-seam metal roof floats above the stone base, supported by tendrils of steel to create a clerestory that lets light filter in. Richly colored fieldstone echoes the warm hue of the soil predominant in the Cotulla area.

To create a contrasting experience to the expansive river views, Lake/Flato combined low-slung, stucco sheds used for bedrooms and a steel "truck arbor" to surround a semi-arid courtyard. Flanked by a stock tank, a breezeway completes the courtyard and cools the summer winds as they pass through to the adjacent rooms. Opposite the main room at the end of the house, a long, arcing screened room overlooks the open pasture.

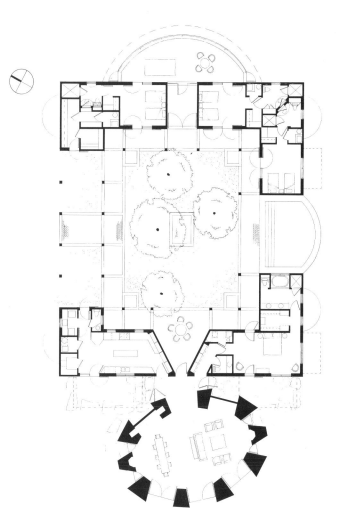

The living room pavilion is angled to take advantage of views to the Nueces River. The stock tank breezeway and the semi-circular screened porch allow air flow into the courtyard while keeping the wildlife out.

Fernandes Residence

MARBLE FALLS, TEXAS

The oak-covered site for the Fernandes house is on a projecting point of land on a central Texas lake. The clients wanted privacy amid the dense development of the surrounding shoreline, and they needed to accommodate frequent guests and grown children.

To isolate the point from the surrounding neighbors, Lake/Flato conceived the house as a series of small-scaled independent structures with distinct shapes that serve to define the perimeter of the private inner courtyard. The structures include a long stone garage building, a squat guest house with lift-up louvers, an elevated sleeping pavilion and boat shelter, and the main house. Porches connect the separate structures to the central hall of the main house, which leads to the prow of the compound—a grand main room—set on a jetty formed from massive, locally quarried granite boulders to stabilize and enhance the natural shoreline of the point.

Like 19th-century farmhouses, the main house has rooms on either side of the central hallway with operable transoms above their doors to draw ventilation in from the hall and through the rooms. The axis of the central hall extends into the courtyard as a linear pool with a wider communal circle inserted at its middle. Views from the house make visitors feel as though they are perched on the edge of the water. The granite of the jetty flows inside and joins a palette of concrete, white oak, limestone, and stucco. Flooring throughout is an elegant second layer of concrete, poured into a oak grid and coated with kerosene and linseed oil. Monolithic limestone frames the fireplace and a collection of Arts & Crafts-inspired furniture provide a warm environment as visitors look out across the expansive blue water.

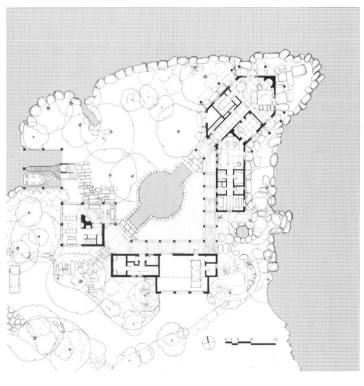

The main living area's "jetty" porches are designed as an extension of the natural waterfront while the granite pavers give the inner courtyard porches a more ordered design. Granite boulders from a nearby quarry were used to shore up the water's edge.

Arsenal Street House

The Arsenal Street House—the first new urban residential project by Lake/Flato—is located on the banks of the San Antonio River, in the historic King William district near downtown San Antonio. The clients, an artist/art dealer and stockbroker with college-aged children, wanted to create an environment that would enhance their ever-changing art collection and take advantage of the impressive views of the river and downtown San Antonio.

With a lot that was only fifty feet square, Lake/Flato took the building straight up. Design cues came from neighboring industrial buildings. The house is broken into three simple volumes, emphasizing its verticality, while expressing the functions contained within. The central, main vertical element houses bedrooms and living areas. To one side, embracing the river, is the open stucco grid of the arbor-covered terrace; to the other, is the third form—a stucco- and sheet-metal-banded "service core," which contains the grand stair, kitchen, and master bath. The stairs wind up from the entry to the main gallery living space on the second level, which is elevated above the nearby street and overlooks the river. Continuing up, the master bath comprises the third floor; while the fourth floor master bedroom penthouse features two decks for river viewing and a vaulted ceiling whose curved profile caps the central four-story stucco tower.

LEVEL ONE

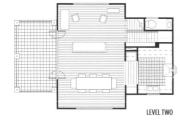

LEVEL TWO

LEVEL THREE

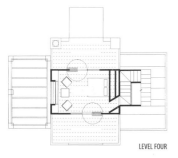

LEVEL FOUR

The interior of the structure is gypsum board on wood studs with inexpensive finishes, including plywood, roof trusses, sheet metal, and galvanized pipe, to introduce a rich texture. Placing the living room and kitchen on the second floor provides privacy from the busy street while taking advantage of views to the San Antonio riverwalk and the city.

Lasater Residence

FORT WORTH, TEXAS

As with their ranch house at La Barronena, the Lasaters wanted to be connected to the outdoors on this in-town site. After discussing how to open the house to natural settings, the Lasaters and Flato traveled to Japan to refine their sensibilities about the relationship of gardens to buildings.

The Lasater House is located in an old Fort Worth neighborhood on a heavily wooded, sloping site overlooking the wide Trinity River Valley. To take advantage of the natural characteristics and orientation of the site, the design began with the exterior spaces. The site was broken into a series of "streets" with enclosed courtyards and open spaces defined by walls clad in large, irregular-shaped pieces of native limestone set with wide, flush mortar. The streets follow a gradual, open-air descent from the garage and main entry, past private portions of the house, to the glass and white oak public pavilions that float above the lush native landscape at the lower end of the site. Sheltered by a series of deep awnings supported by a delicate steel structure, the pavilions surround the courts and open to views and prevailing breezes. Bedrooms and private areas of the house are recessed into the sloping site and appear not as built areas, but as thick, low-scaled limestone walls. Bisecting the triangular site with the residence created two distinctively different gardens: a shade garden that works with the large trees and native vegetation, and a garden of soft grasses that overlooks the broad river valley. The planting creeps into the rigorously ordered spaces, softening the planar structures and merging grounds with buildings, enhancing the sense that the pavilions have naturally emerged from the woods.

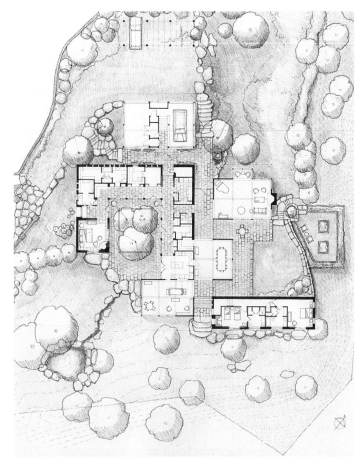

Flanking both sides of the narrow entry "street," low-scaled limestone walls hide the master bedroom and garage. The walls are banded with grey stone to break up their scale and imitate the natural layering process of limestone.

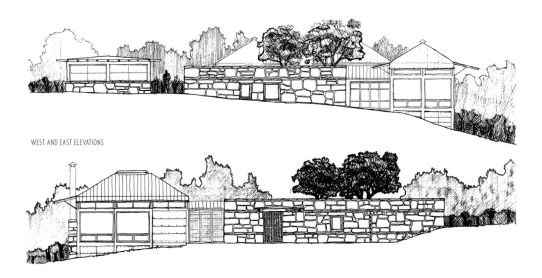

WEST AND EAST ELEVATIONS

The main living areas, inside the
wood, glass, and copper pavilions,
open on one side to a formal gravel
courtyard enclosed by the low walls
of the guest bedrooms while floating
above an expansive natural garden
on the other side.

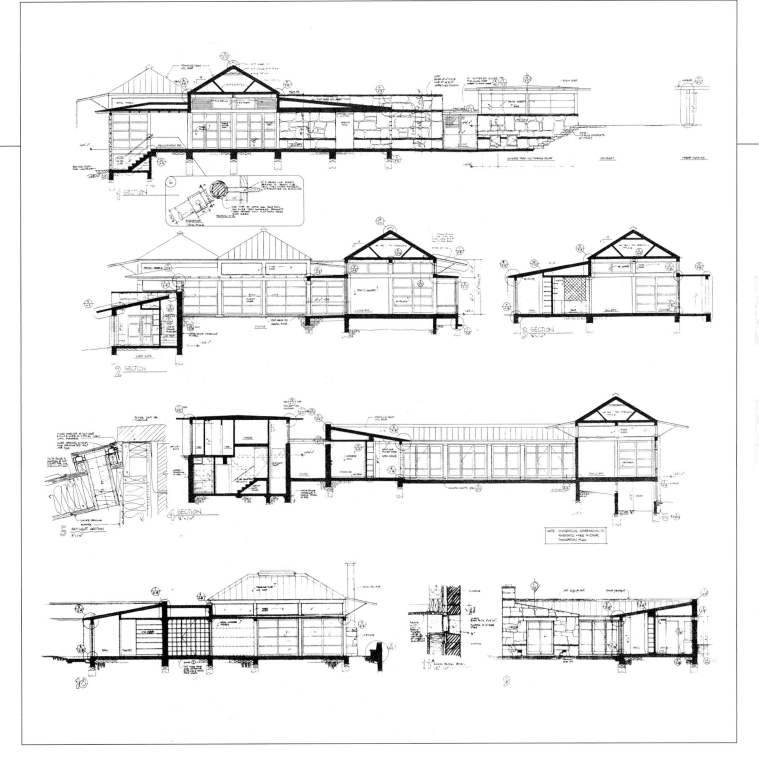

The finely finished white oak beams, columns and infill panels of the pavilion's interior create a strong contrast to the primitive stone walls and floor of the "exterior streets" which continue through the interiors of the house.

Elm Court Residence

SAN ANTONIO, TEXAS

The client, a prominent gallery owner in San Antonio, wanted a house with a studio for working on her own sculpture, enough walls to exhibit her large collection of contemporary art, and outdoor spaces for sculpture. The site, which is bordered on one side by an old allee of beautiful oak trees and on the other by an existing tennis court, was organized into a series of courtyards. At the center, a 30' x 30' sculpture court is encircled by a main gallery with large walls for art and high clerestory windows for abundant light. In the more private rooms off the gallery, cupolas bring in rich, indirect light. The structures are a study in contrast; light-steel lantern-like roofs rest gingerly on heavy, grounded volumes clad in monumental blocks of Hill Country limestone. Inside, white oak floors provide a consistent warm, soft-looking ground in contrast to the cooler stone. Though the urban site contrasts dramatically with the firm's earlier South Texas ranch house settings, the similar courtyard organization works as well here to gather in landscape and open rooms to the outdoors. Breezeways between the rooms that enclose the central courtyard connect with other outdoor spaces and create an expansive sense on the narrow lot.

In the backyard, a narrow, sunny pool courtyard is bordered by two steel-framed studios. The allee of trees on the west side is the central focus of a shade-loving garden. To the east, a truck access for the studios takes the form of a "green street" separating the garage from the main house.

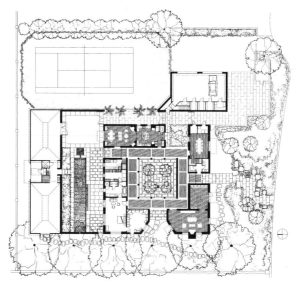

The light metal roof forms sit gingerly atop massive stone walls which are used to break the house site into a series of courtyards and green "streets." Primitive uncut stone boulders line the walk to the house, contrasting with the honed character of the walls.

The house has a number of exterior rooms, which soften the architecture and help erase the line between indoors and out. Cupolas provide indirect light to the pavilions while metal sun shades protect the windows.

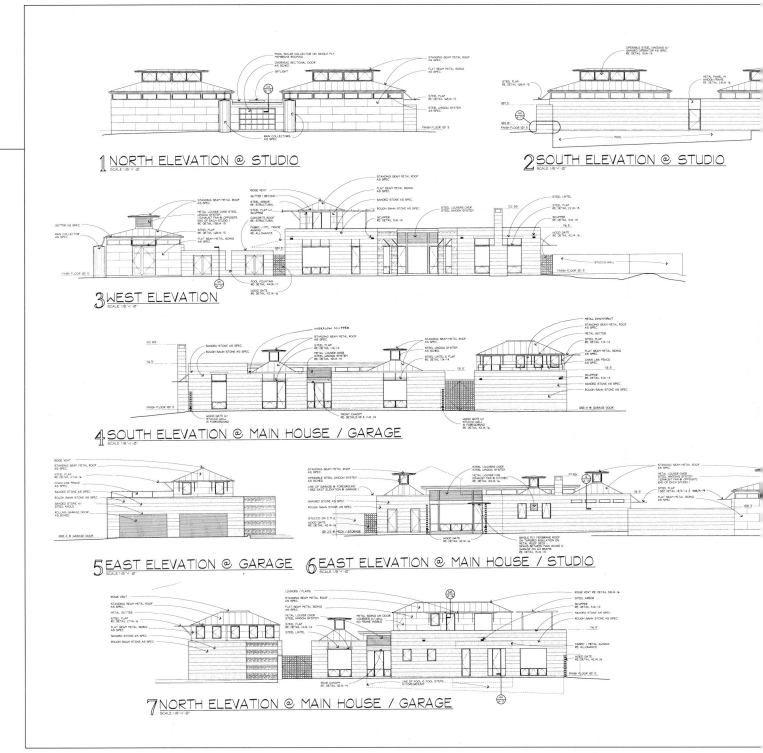

1 NORTH ELEVATION @ STUDIO
SCALE 1/8"=1'-0"

2 SOUTH ELEVATION @ STUDIO
SCALE 1/8"=1'-0"

3 WEST ELEVATION
SCALE 1/8"=1'-0"

4 SOUTH ELEVATION @ MAIN HOUSE / GARAGE
SCALE 1/8"=1'-0"

5 EAST ELEVATION @ GARAGE
SCALE 1/8"=1'-0"

6 EAST ELEVATION @ MAIN HOUSE / STUDIO
SCALE 1/8"=1'-0"

7 NORTH ELEVATION @ MAIN HOUSE / GARAGE
SCALE 1/8"=1'-0"

STANDING SEAM METAL ROOF
AS SPEC.

METAL GUTTER
AS SPEC.

STEEL WINDOW SYSTEM
AS SCHED.

SANDED STONE AS SPEC.

ROUGH SAWN STONE AS SPEC.

FINISH FLOOR 121.5

EXISTING COURT ELEV. 119.4

METAL GUTTER
AS SPEC.

RAIN COLLECTOR
AS SPEC.

FINISH FLOOR 121.5

The central gallery has a variety of light and spatial qualities, allowing it to work for the display of sculpture and art. The gallery surrounds the central court, linking it to the front door and the major outdoor spaces.

Carraro Residence

KYLE, TEXAS

When the Carraros came to Lake/Flato with a tight budget and big dreams about large, barn-like loft spaces, the architects suggested looking at the Alamo Cement Plant in San Antonio, which had been abandoned and was being demolished for future residential and commercial development. For years, Lake/Flato had admired the Modernist aesthetic of the elegant 1920s steel-framed structures. Although the plant's immense scale made most of the buildings unfit for residential use, the Carraros were receptive to the idea of reusing the smallest structure on the site, a 40 x 180 x 20-foot-high shed. The structure was disassembled and trucked to the site south of Austin, a heavily wooded ranch on forty acres in the Texas Hill Country.

The Carraro house celebrates the beauty of industrial architecture. The steel building is divided into three parts: the narrow central building is clad in galvanized metal and contains the master bedroom, library, utility, and open dog-run entry; the open, three-bay structure is the garage and farm implement building; the four-bay structure contains the limestone walls that form the living room, kitchen, and second-story guest room, which floats within the full-height screened walls, and shelters the large outdoor room from winter winds. The clerestory above, with a full-length skylight of corrugated fiberglass, dissipates the perceived enclosure of the roof and, with walls of uninterrupted horizontal screen bands, establishes a sense of being in the open landscape. The overall arrangement of the buildings works with the oak trees to create two distinctive courtyards—an entry court defined by the open pavilion and a river court defined by the screened building.

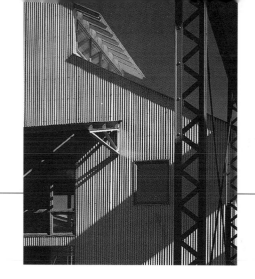

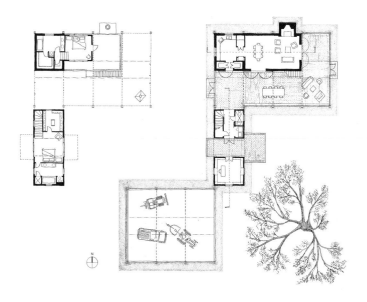

(Opposite page, above) The early
20th-century Alamo Cement
Warehouse structure was recycled for
the house, a collage of materials that
celebrate the simple beauty of the
steel frame: flat and corrugated metal,
horizontal screen bands, native limestone walls and recycled kiln brick.

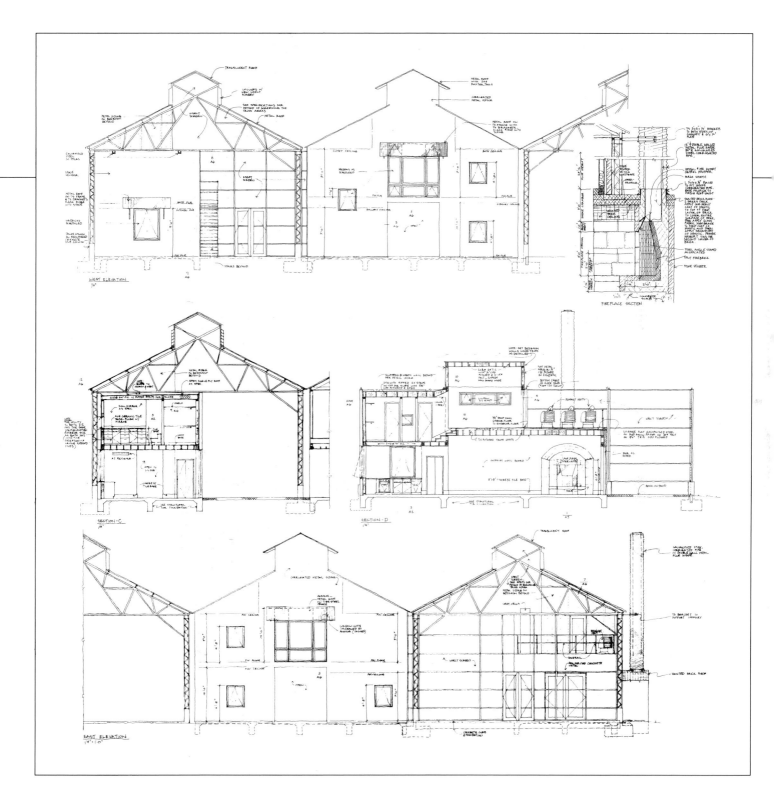

Oriented to the cool summer breezes, the two-story screen room is sheltered from the winter winds by the stone living room and "light" metal-clad second-story guest room. Accessed by a light steel stair, an upper deck allows for a second-floor experience within the great screen room.

Great Northwest Branch Library

SAN ANTONIO, TEXAS

This branch library for the City of San Antonio is located in a suburban area where the open, flat, South Texas plain meets the tree-covered, limestone-rich hill country. The client required a 12,000-square-foot plan that could be easily expanded. The location of the building and parking allows for a future wing which will create an L-shaped plan.

Located at an intersection of wide streets, Lake/Flato placed the entrance of the library away from the road toward the heart of the neighborhood, ensuring a sense of community. Simple, indigenous building forms were used to reinforce the no-nonsense nature of the library. The bookstack areas, which are generally quieter, are in the low, limestone walls, while high, vaulted roofs with clerestory windows denote zones of public activity. The interior of the building expresses its industrial roots with exposed steel framing, plywood panels, wood trusses, metal roof decks, exposed mechanical ducts, and utilitarian light fixtures.

On the street side, the building has a series of courtyard niches in the stone wall. Combined with operable louvers, the niches work as shading devices for the glass reading room beyond. The mechanical units, located in the outside louvered areas, mask street sounds with white noise and also serve a practical

ornamentation, working in tandem with the big letters that announce the building. An example of assembling a building by repeating simple organizational units, the library combines alternating solids and voids to create a varied and rich interior space, yet a simple kit for future expansion.

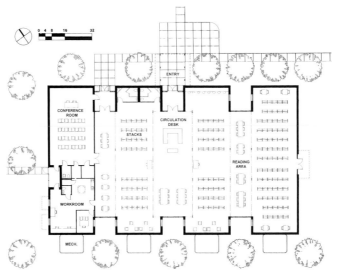

CONFERENCE ROOM	ENTRY
STACKS	CIRCULATION DESK
WORKROOM	READING AREA
MECH.	

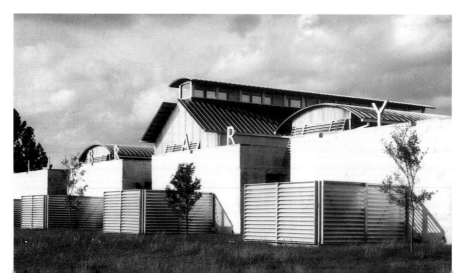

The opaque stone-walled volumes house the books, and the open pavilions bring light to the reading rooms. A series of breaks in the solid stone wall create an intimate garden experience for the glass-walled reading rooms.

Holt Corporate Headquarters

SAN ANTONIO, TEXAS

When Lake/Flato was asked to design the headquarters of Holt Companies (a major San Antonio distributor of Caterpillar tractors), it seized the opportunity to reinterpret the prefabricated metal building forms found on the 15-acre company campus. In addition to required office spaces, the design was to incorporate the company's collection of paintings, sculpture, and antique tractors.

Using a prefabricated metal structure allowed Lake/Flato to meet the client's rapid design and construction schedule, to match the existing scale of the campus, and to introduce a modular plan that fit the regimented program of offices and meeting spaces. The building, finished in galvanized aluminum and a standard aluminum window system, is fitted around clusters of mature oak trees that, along with the buildings, create two distinct courtyards. The public entry side of the building is bounded by the "tractor" porch, while the rear courtyard contains the "sculpture" porch. The porches and clerestories act as large shading devices for the glass-enclosed painting galleries. Offices open off the gallery hallways and have views out to the trees and the ever-changing tractor inventory.

Commenting on the design, architect William Turnbull said, "the building is strong and industrial, like the tractors, and it is suggestive of the early International Style pavilions in its 'machinery-as-art' theme."

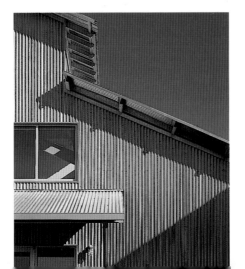

1 RECEPTION
2 OFFICES
3 SECOND-FLOOR
  CONFERENCE ROOM
4 TRACTOR PORCH
5 SCULPTURE PORCH
6 PARKING

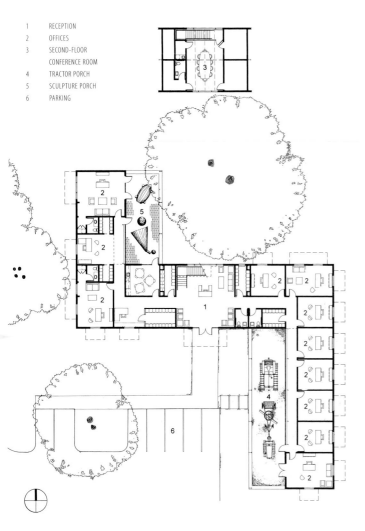

The office hallway, which also serves as an art gallery, is shaded by the tall metal porch that protects the antique tractors outside. The glazed, sloped ceiling of the gallery lets in rich indirect light.

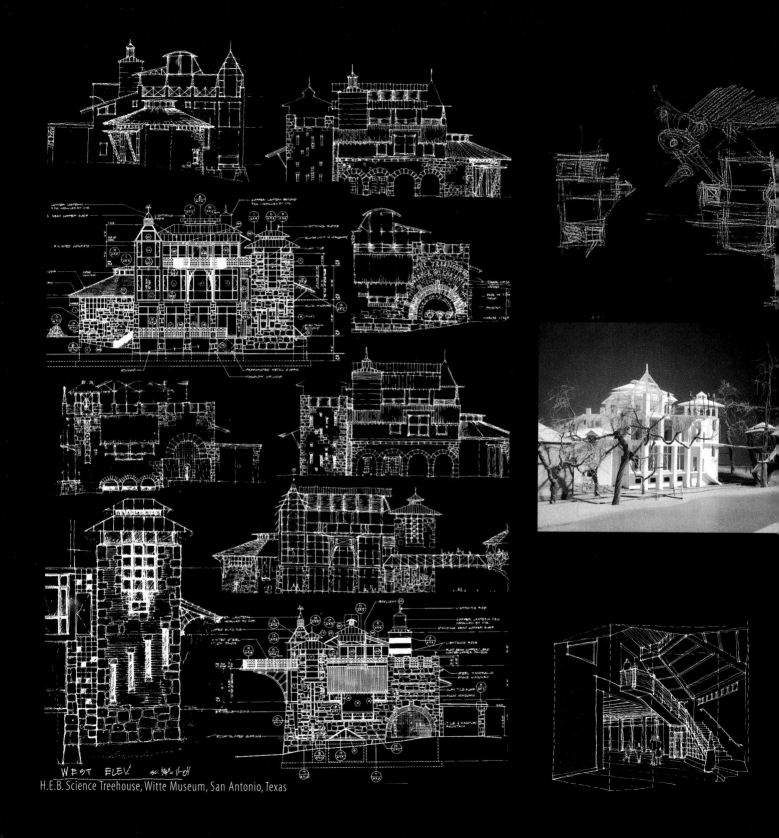

H.E.B. Science Treehouse, Witte Museum, San Antonio, Texas

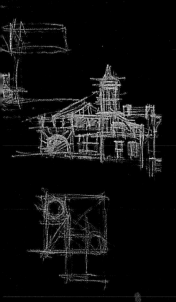

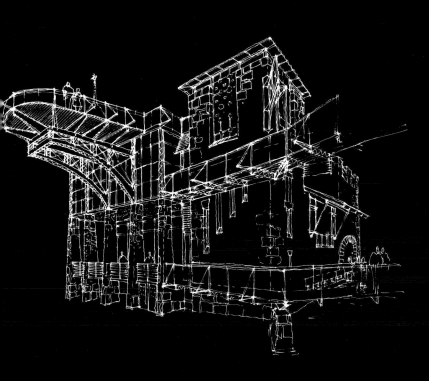

In Progress ▶

Garden of the Gods Club

The Garden of the Gods Park is a red sandstone formation that reaches to the sky with dynamic shapes in front of Pikes Peak in Colorado Springs. The private Garden of the Gods club has a salon, spa, dining room, and meeting rooms, as well as fifty hotel rooms. The 80,000-square-foot building steps along a plateau edge that runs north-south and overlooks the Garden of the Gods Park and Pikes Peak, enabling each room to share the spectacular views.

The 950-foot-long west elevation is dominated by the clubhouse gable roof, reminiscent of the original clubhouse of the 1950s, and further inspired by the rustic lodges and simple mining structures found in Colorado. Battered, red sandstone piers provide order to the meandering plan. Similar in form and color to the Garden of the Gods rocks, these stone piers become walls running east-west to help frame the view, distinguishing the spaces of the lobby, bar, and dining room. A sixteen-foot-deep porch runs the length of the clubhouse to provide shade from the western sun while encouraging outdoor dining and entertainment. Piers, balconies, porches, overhangs, and arbors all combine to cast shadows on the long facades, interrupting the linear architecture. Gables and sheds create a varied array of volumes and spaces.

Just as Texas' limestone and its humble agricultural buildings inspire Lake/Flato's architecture in that state, the astounding weathered sandstone formations and early mining towns and even ancient Anasazi dwellings generate a new vocabulary for building that fits a different landscape.

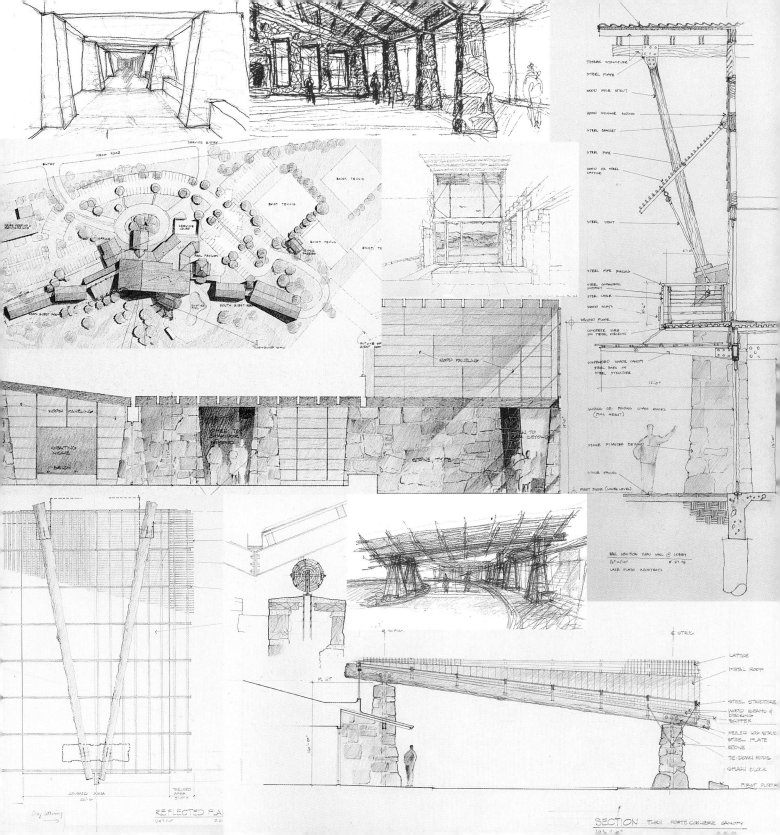

SECTION THRU PORTE-COCHERE CANOPY

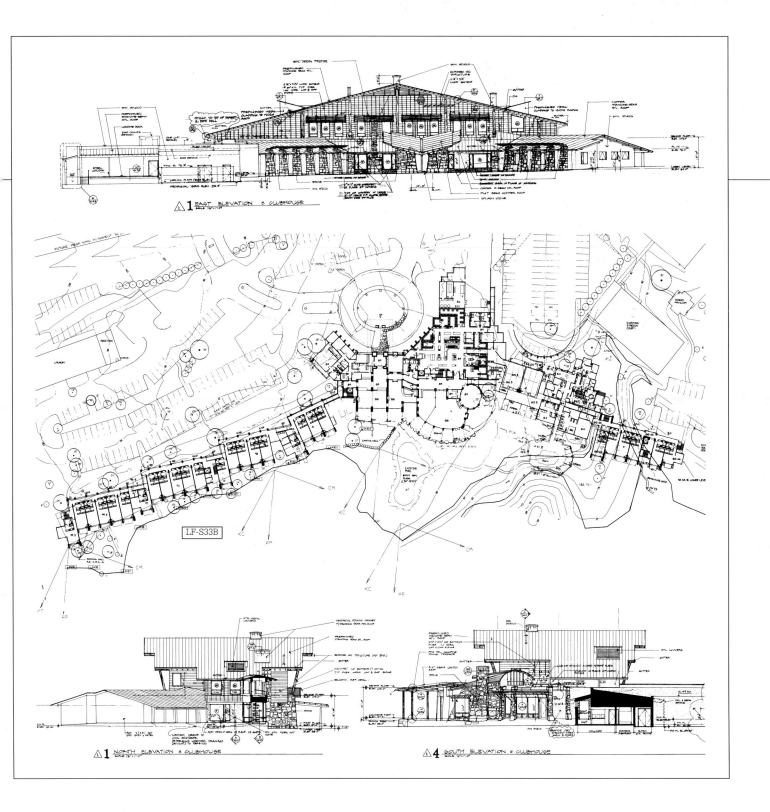

△ 1 EAST ELEVATION @ CLUBHOUSE

LF-S33B

△ 1 NORTH ELEVATION @ CLUBHOUSE

△ 4 SOUTH ELEVATION @ CLUBHOUSE

Burlington Northern Santa Fe

FORT WORTH, TEXAS

Brick buildings of Fort Worth and the rural architecture of North Texas provided the architectural
character of Lake/Flato's design for Burlington Northern Santa Fe Railroad's 180-acre site master plan.
To preserve the prairie landscape, the rural campus is organized by an arcing boulevard, serpentine
berm, tree bands, and a prairie commons. The first phase, a 140,000-square-foot network control center
for tracking trains across the nation and companion 80,000-square-foot office building, was under way
when Lake/Flato was hired to design structures and use materials that would animate these buildings
and create a cohesive architectural character for future building.

Brick, metal, and concrete form a practical and rugged building palette for the railroad. Handsome brick
buildings across Fort Worth, for instance, encompass uses from stockyards and warehouses to early-
twentieth-century commercial buildings, and concrete grain silos mark the Texas landscape and
Burlington's routes. The precast concrete panels for the control center reflect the board-formed texture
of silos and reinforce the tornado-proof nature of this building. Galvanized metal, commonly found on
light industrial buildings, train stations, canopies, barns, and sheds, provides the roofs of the office
buildings, held aloft with steel struts to create a 16-foot overhang. The strong horizontal shadow this
creates gives weight to the buildings and roots them to the broad prairie horizon. The contrast between
heavy masonry and light steel construction builds upon the legacy of railroad architecture.

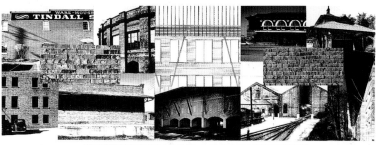

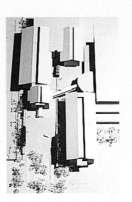

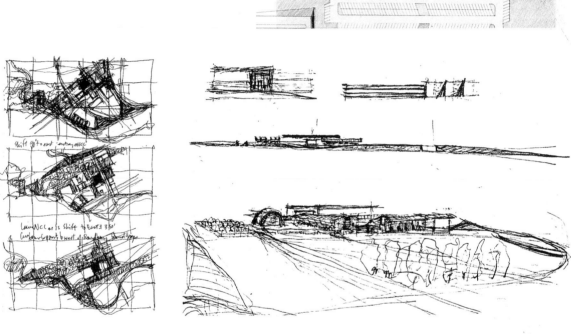

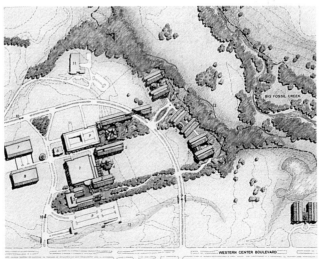

The office buildings are oriented east-west to minimize west exposure, orienting views into linear courtyards and then out beyond to the expansive prairie horizon. These narrow shed buildings connect to the entry building, whose grand arch and lofty interior lobby recall the old Fort Worth Santa Fe train station. (Overleaf) The Network Control Center is tornado-proof, has no windows, and is punctuated by the steel plate louvers that protect the mechanical equipment.

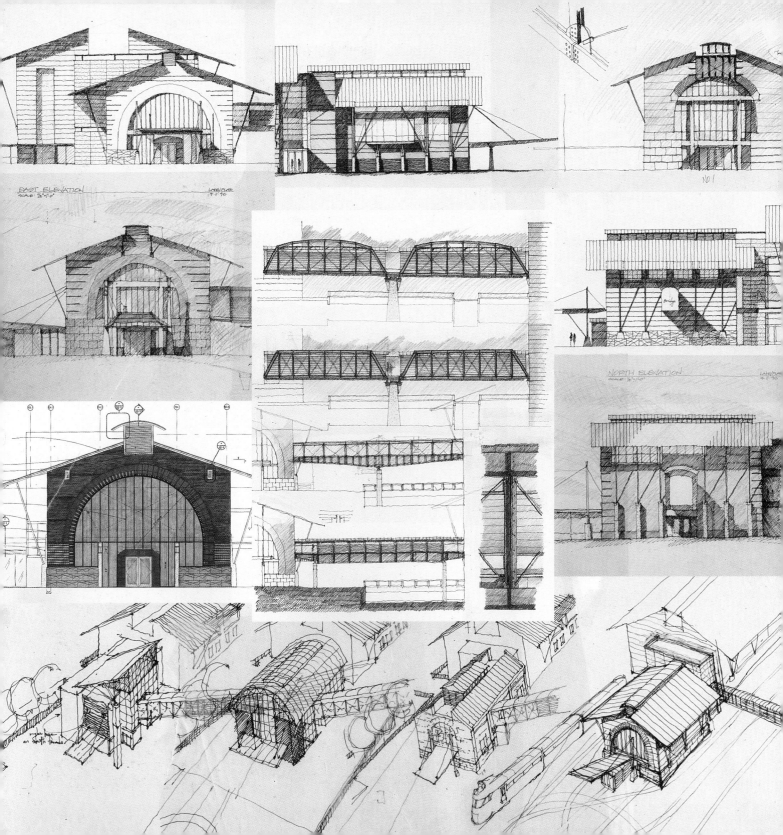

EAST ELEVATION
SCALE 1/6"=1'-0"   LANDPLATE
                                    14-11-90

NORTH ELEVATION
SCALE 1/6"=1'-0"   LANDPLATE
                                   4-11-90

NO/

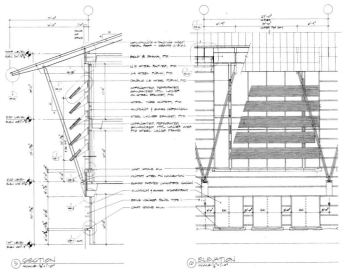

⑤ SECTION
SCALE 1/8" = 1'-0"

⑥ ELEVATION
SCALE 1/8" = 1'-0"

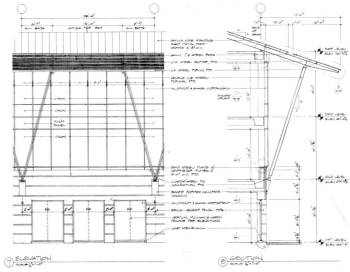

⑦ ELEVATION
SCALE 1/8" = 1'-0"

⑧ SECTION
SCALE 1/8" = 1'-0"

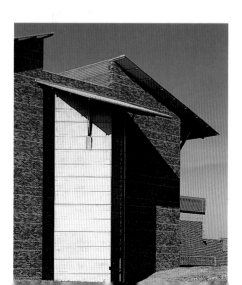

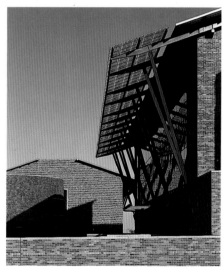

The precast concrete skin on the Network Control Center emulates the texture and color of the nearby concrete silos. The metal "cornice" above the concrete has the scale and rhythm of rail cars. The office building has a sixteen-foot opaque overhang on the south and a sun screen on the north so direct light and heat gain are controlled.

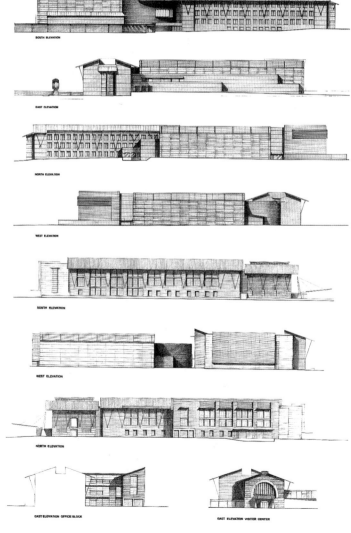

SOUTH ELEVATION

EAST ELEVATION

NORTH ELEVATION

WEST ELEVATION

SOUTH ELEVATION

WEST ELEVATION

NORTH ELEVATION

EAST ELEVATION OFFICE BLOCK

EAST ELEVATION VISITOR CENTER

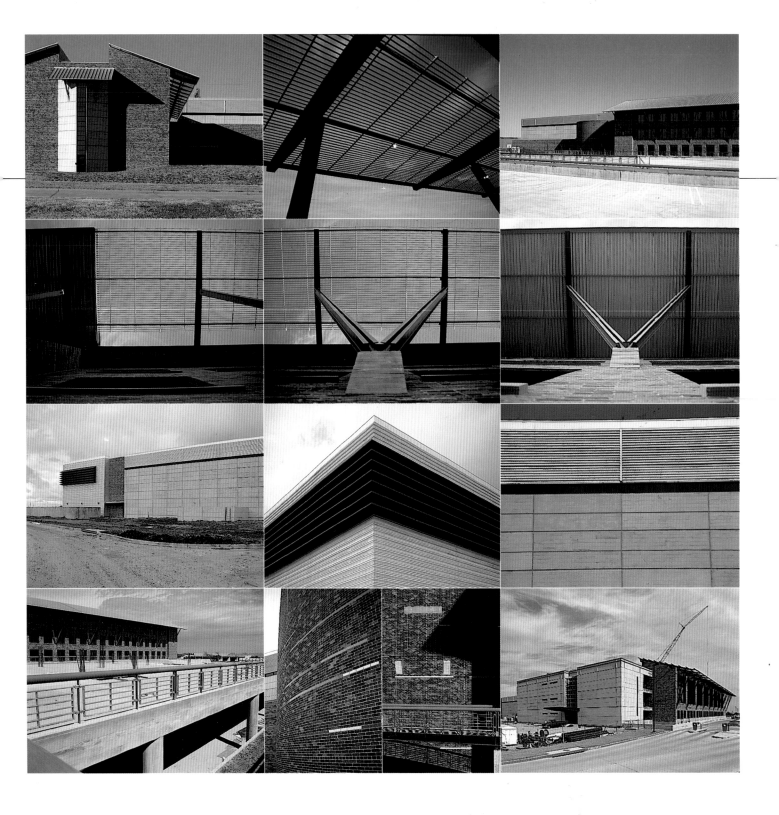

Texas State Cemetery

AUSTIN, TEXAS

Founded in 1851, the Texas Sate Cemetery is located in an old neighborhood east of the capitol. Lake/Flato and landscape architect Jim Keeter developed a master plan to restore the cemetery.

The design reduces the architecture to simple walls, which elegantly enclose the naturally beautiful site. This is the "thick wall" distilled to its essence, simultaneously solid and void, space itself and definer of space. The long limestone wall of the Visitor Center serves as office and gallery. Visitors enter the cemetery through the breezeway with views to Crescent Lake and Oakview. The columbarium (a linear mausoleum) is a curving granite wall whose Rose Gate is the ceremonial portal to the cemetery. From this gate, the oak allee leads to the Plaza of Memory, which pays tribute to Texans not buried in the cemetery.

The original rural landscape of native grasses and wildflowers will be restored to keep the spirit of other rural Texas cemeteries. A new cypress pool and crescent lake will flow past native sycamores and cypress trees like a central Texas stream. Oakview, the tallest hill, will be raised 10 feet by fill from the ponds to afford a view of the Capitol and be shaded by a lone oak, the sentry of the cemetery. Given new meaning with these additions and the restoration of the grounds, the Texas State Cemetery will take its spiritual place in the state's lore and history that Arlington National Cemetery holds for the nation.

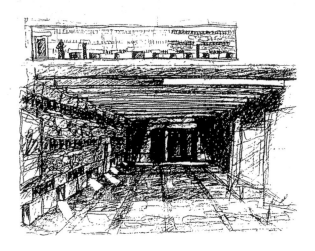

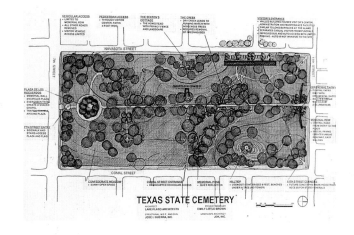

VEHICULAR ACCESS
• LIMITED TO MEMORIAL ROW
• ALL OTHER ROADS REMOVED
• VISITOR VEHICLE ACCESS LIMITED

PEDESTRIAN ACCESS
• THROUGH VISITOR CENTER, PATHS
• 4 FOOT WIDE

THE SEATON'S COTTAGE
• THE HOMESTEAD WITH PRIVACY FENCE AND LANDSCAPE

THE CREEK
• DRY CREEK LEADS TO RUNNING WATER WITH INDIGENOUS TREES
• REQUIRES REMOVAL OF GREENHOUSES

VISITOR'S ENTRANCE
• WALLED BUILDING HOUSES VISITOR'S CENTER, ADMINISTRATION AND MAINTENANCE FACILITIES
• SIMILAR TO LONG BARRACKS AT THE ALAMO
• SEPARATES CASUAL VISITOR FROM FUNERALS
• IMPROVED BUS AND AUTO ACCESS WITH LIMITED PARKING - AUTO IS NOT INVASIVE TO THE SITE

PLAZA DE LOS RECUERDOS
• MEMORIAL WALL ENCIRCLES PLAZA
• EVERGREEN TREES CREATE A SHADED CHAPEL
• TRAFFIC MOVES AROUND PLAZA

CEREMONIAL ENTRY
• FORMAL ENTRY
• GATE WITH CEREMONIAL GATES
• TERRACE WALK LEADING TO COLUMBARIUM

7TH STREET ENTRY
• SIDEWALK AND STAIRS ACCESS PLAZA AND FLAG

MEMORIAL ROW
• CENTRAL ROAD FROM ENTRY TO THE PLAZA
• CREATES UNIQUE HEADSTONES AND ROW ALONG IT

CONFEDERATE MEADOW
• SUNNY OPEN SPACE

COMAL STREET ENTRANCE
• HANDICAPPED VEHICULAR ACCESS

MEMORIAL POND
• QUIET REFLECTION

HILLTOP
• LOOKOUT CONTAINED 4 FEET, BENCHES UNDER A TREE (NO TOWER)

11TH STREET CORNER
• FUTURE CENOTAPHS MARK PEDESTRIAN ACCESS AS FOR STATE FUNERALS

TEXAS STATE CEMETERY

ARCHITECT
LAKE/FLATO ARCHITECTS

PROJECT MANAGER
EMILY LITTLE BROWN

STRUCTURAL, ME P. AND CIVIL
JOSE I. GUERRA, INC.

LANDSCAPE ARCHITECT
JEW, INC.

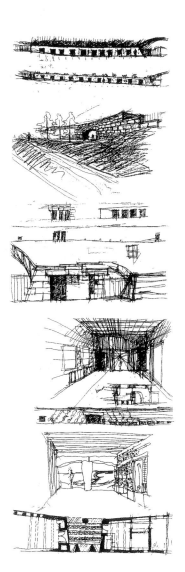

(Below) The existing cemetery lacks the walled enclosure found in most Texas cemeteries. The Memorial Way is a processional road, leading the visitor past the Crescent Pool, Oakview, Confederate field, and Republic Hill to the Plaza of Memory, a round space enclosed by large irregular boulders and small dry-stacked stones, similar to an old field stone wall.

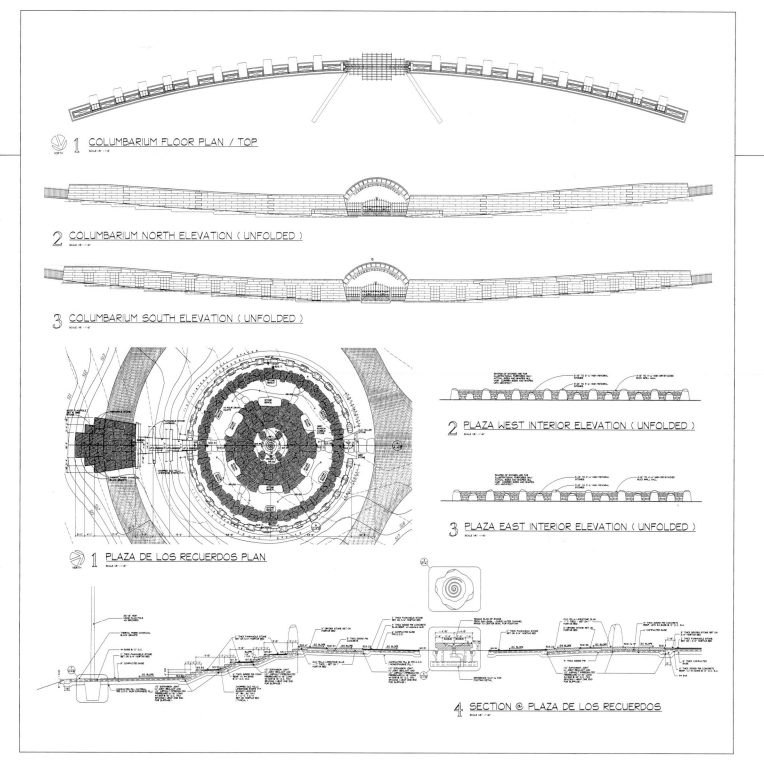

1 COLUMBARIUM FLOOR PLAN / TOP
SCALE 1/8" = 1'-0"

2 COLUMBARIUM NORTH ELEVATION (UNFOLDED)
SCALE 1/8" = 1'-0"

3 COLUMBARIUM SOUTH ELEVATION (UNFOLDED)
SCALE 1/8" = 1'-0"

2 PLAZA WEST INTERIOR ELEVATION (UNFOLDED)
SCALE 1/8" = 1'-0"

3 PLAZA EAST INTERIOR ELEVATION (UNFOLDED)
SCALE 1/8" = 1'-0"

1 PLAZA DE LOS RECUERDOS PLAN
SCALE 1/8" = 1'-0"

4 SECTION @ PLAZA DE LOS RECUERDOS
SCALE 1/8" = 1'-0"

Santa Fe House II

The client wanted a house with places for art and spaces filled with light. "I might even want to sleep in the gallery on a couch right next to the art," she told the architects.

Unlike the first Lake/Flato Santa Fe house, sited on a steep site in the Historic District, this house is south of the city, on a large, open, rural-feeling tract. And unlike the first house, which spatially revolved around a variety of adobe shapes, this house centers upon the intersection of two distinct spaces. The introspective tall gallery has no external views. Indirect natural light washes its north wall and is balanced by reflected light off the adobe wall. The extroverted long room has views to the south, west, and north through tall doorways and low windows. A bridge overlooking the solar greenhouse travels across the sunken gallery of the tall room and along a curving adobe wall, linking the bedroom to the long living space. Wide, floor-to-ceiling pocket walls slide open to strengthen the concept of a house for light and space, blurring the idea of separate rooms in favor of a house with two spaces. Away from the tall gallery, the intimate scaled spaces evoke the low-slung pueblos of the area. The scale and massing of the exterior recalls the opaque character of an old adobe church; it blends the house with the neighborhood and disguises the modern space within.

mud plaster walls w/ art - and the
white room

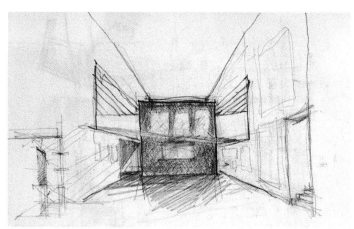

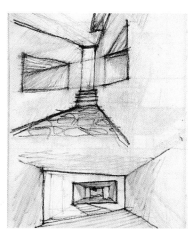

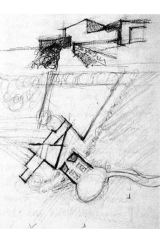

Appendix ▶

Selected Works

1984-1996

1	2	3	
4	5	6	7
8	9	10	11
12		13	
14		15	

16	17	18	19	20
21	22	25		26
23	24	27		28
29	30	31	32	33	34	35
36	37	38	39	40	41

List of Works and Credits

SANTA FE HOUSE I; Santa Fe, New Mexico, 1990
Awards: 1990-State Honor Award, Texas Society of Architects
Architect Team: David Lake, Ted Flato, John Grable, Robert Trinidad
Structural: HKS Engineering (Jim Kreis, Jim Hands)
Contractor: Adobe Corporation (Robert Taylor)
Photographers: Bill Kennedy; David Lake

LA BARRONENA RANCH; Hebbronville, Texas, 1986
Awards: 1986-State Honor Award, Texas Society of Architects
Client: Mollie and Garland Lasater
Architect Team: Ford Powell & Carson
Principal in charge: Chris Carson
Design Team: Ted Flato, Lynette Polari
Contractor: Phillip Storm
Photographers: Jon Jensen: Reprinted with the permission of Metropolitan
Home Magazine, Hachette Fillipacchi USA Inc.; Lake/Flato

SOUTH BURKE RANCH; Zavala County, Texas, 1987
Awards: 1989-State Honor Award, Texas Society of Architects
Architect Team: Ted Flato, David Lake, Graham Martin
Structural: Reynolds-Slattner-Chetter-Roll Inc.
Contractor: George Geis
Photographers: David Lake, Graham Martin

LA ESTRELLA RANCH; Roma, Texas, 1989
Client: Tommy Funk
Awards: 1993-National Brick Award, AIA
1991-State Honor Award, Texas Society of Architects
Architect Team: David Lake, Ted Flato, Graham Martin
Contractor: Charles Scott
Photographers: Blackmon Winters Inc.; David Lake

CARTER RANCH; Millican, Texas, 1990
Awards: 1993-State Honor Award, Texas Society of Architects
Client: Jack Carter
Architect Team: Ted Flato, David Lake, John Grable, Scott Glenn
Contractor: Custom Homes Inc. (Mark Robinson)
Photographer: © 1995 Hester+Hardaway, Fayetteville, Texas;
Reprinted with the permission of Metropolitan Home Magazine

EL TULE RANCH; Falfurrias, Texas, 1992
Awards: 1992-State Honor Award, Texas Society of Architects
Architect Team: Ted Flato, David Lake, Joaquin Escamilla
Contractor: Timbercon Construction
Photographers: Courtesy HG. © 1993 by the Conde Nast Publications Inc.;
Blackmon Winters Inc.

SALGE LAKE HOUSE; Canyon Lake, Texas, 1989
Awards: 1989-State Honor Award, Texas Society of Architects
Client: Debra Salge
Architect Team: Ted Flato, David Lake, John Grable
Contractor: Jimmie Penshorn
Photographers: David Lake, Eric Buck

CHANDLER RANCH; Mason, Texas, 1993
Architect Team: David Lake, Ted Flato, John Grable, Robert Trinidad
Client: Mark Chandler
Interiors: June Chandler
Landscape: Jim Keeter, ASLA
Contractor: Henry Duecker
Photographers: Reprinted by permission of HOUSE BEAUTIFUL, copyright
November 1992. All rights reserved. Timothy Hursley, photographer

COTULLA RANCH; Cotulla Texas, 1996
Architect Team: Ted Flato, David Lake, Graham Martin
Interiors: Courtney Walker, ASID
Contractor: Koehler Company
Photographer: Graham Martin, Javier Huerta

FERNANDES RESIDENCE; Marble Falls, Texas, 1990
Client: Sandra and Gary Fernandes
Architect Team: Ted Flato, David Lake, Scott Glenn
Structural: Reynolds-Slattner-Chetter-Roll Inc.
Mechanical/Electrical: Barry Engineers
Interiors: Lake/Flato and M. Robbins Black
Landscape: Jim Keeter
Contractor: Koehler Construction
Photographer: Antoine Bootz: Reprinted with the permission of
Metropolitan Home Magazine, Hachette Fillipacchi USA Inc.

ARSENAL STREET HOUSE; San Antonio, Texas, 1989
Architect Team: Ted Flato, David Lake, Graham Martin
Contractor: Twin Tech
Photographer: Reprinted by permission of HOUSE BEAUTIFUL, © November
1992. All rights reserved. Timothy Hursley, photographer.

LASATER RESIDENCE; Fort Worth, Texas
Awards: 1995-State Honor Award, Texas Society of Architects
Client: Mr. & Mrs. Garland Lasater
Architect Team: Ted Flato, David Lake, Karla Greer
Lighting: John Bos; Jane & Graham Martin (Custom Light Fixtures)
Interiors: David Corley
Landscape: Kings Creek Landscaping Inc.
Contractor: JBM Builders Inc.
Photographer: Michael Lyon, David Lake

ELM COURT RESIDENCE; San Antonio, Texas, 1995
Architect Team: Ted Flato, David Lake, Graham Martin, Robert Trinidad
Structural: Reynolds-Schlattner-Chetter-Roll Inc.
Interiors: Courtney Walker, ASID
Landscape: Kings Creek Landscaping Inc.
Contractor: The Koehler Company
Photographer: © 1995 Hester+Hardaway, Fayetteville, Texas

CARRARO RESIDENCE; Kyle, Texas, 1990
Awards: 1993-AIA Western Home Award
1992-AIA National Honor Award
1991-Record Houses Award, Architectural Record
1991-State Honor Award, Texas Society of Architects
Architect Team: Ted Flato, David Lake, Graham Martin
Contractor: Allen Custom Home Inc.
Photographer: © 1995 Hester+Hardaway, Fayetteville, Texas

GREAT NORTHWEST BRANCH LIBRARY; San Antonio, Texas, 1995
Client: San Antonio Public Library
Architect Team: Ted Flato, David Lake, Kim Monroe, Joaquin Escamilla
Structural: S.E.A. Inc.
Contractor: Kunz Construction Company Inc.
Photographer: © 1995 Hester+Hardaway, Fayetteville, Texas

HOLT CORPORATE HEADQUARTERS; San Antonio, Texas, 1994
Awards: 1995-State Honor Award, Texas Society of Architects
Architect Team: Ted Flato, David Lake, Scott Glen, Billy Johnson, Graham Martin
Contractor: Cox Construction Inc.
Photographer: © 1995 Hester+Hardaway, Fayetteville, Texas

H-E-B SCIENCE TREEHOUSE; San Antonio, Texas; in progress
Client: Witte Museum of San Antonio, Texas
Architect Team: David Lake, Ted Flato, Matt Morris, Kim Monroe, K. Brown
Model: Francisco Friday Lopez
Sketches: David Lake, Matt Morris, Graham Martin

GARDEN OF THE GODS CLUB; Colorado Springs, Colorado, in progress
Architect Team: David Lake, Ted Flato, Scott Glen, Matt Morris, Kenneth Brown,
Robert Trinidad, Andrew Gomez, Robert Harris, Eric Buck
Project Manager/Interiors: The Hare Group (Don and Sharon Hare)
Sketches: David Lake, Matt Morris

BURLINGTON NORTHERN SANTE FE; Fort Worth, Texas, in progress
Project Architect: KVG Gideon Toal Inc.
Consulting Design Architect: Lake/Flato; David Lake, Ted Flato, Greg Papay, Bob
Harris, Robert Trinidad, Javier Huerta, Francisco Lopez, Enrique Montenegro,
The Pirate John Blood, Tom Rose, Xavier Gonzalez.
Client: Burlington Northern Santa Fe Railroad
Photographer: Michael Lyon, David Lake, Greg Papay
Model: Francisco Friday Lopez, Javier Huerta, Enrique Montenegro, Louis Sierra
Sketches: David Lake, Greg Papay, The Pirate John Blood, Javier Huerta

TEXAS STATE CEMETERY; Austin, Texas, in progress
Client: Texas Parks and Wildlife Department
Architect Team: David Lake, Ted Flato, John Grable, Robert Trinidad, K. Brown
Landscape: Jim E. Keeter Inc., Pat Schneider
Model: Francisco Friday Lopez, Javier Huerta, Brandi Priest
Sketches: David Lake, John Grable

SANTA FE HOUSE II; Santa Fe, New Mexico, in progress
Architect Team: David Lake, Ted Flato, John Grable, Kenneth Brown, Stealth
Civil Engineer: Red Mountain Engineers Inc. (Jim Kries, Jim Hands)
Photographer: David Lake, John Grable

nfidence in our
ossible without
, and exacting
n, Karla Greer,
r often oblique

ir busy
o to our
den.
Oscar Riera
s, and the
spirit of

l forays
e puzzle
Trinidad,
cisco
Anne Culpepper, Billy Aylor,
Escamilla.

Dedication:

This book is dedicated to O' Neil Ford, who inspired us to love both the art of
building and the many people who make it possible.